CREATING A MULTI-SENSORY
SPIRITUAL GARDEN
IN YOUR SCHOOL

By Shahne Vickery

"Let me learn the lessons you have hidden
in every leaf and rock."

Contents

Introduction   5

Chapter 1 – Seen and unseen   9
Garden Story 1
Sarum St Paul's Church of England Primary School, Salisbury
Working with a professional garden designer   16

Chapter 2 – Sound and silence   21
Garden Story 2
Wool Church of England First School, Wool
A Spiritual Garden: A place set apart for reflection and worship   30

Chapter 3 – Touch and feel   33
Garden Story 3
St Osmund's Catholic Primary School, Salisbury
A whole school project to develop the outside space   40

Chapter 4 – Scent and sensing   43
Garden Story 4
Beechcroft St Paul's Church of England Primary School, Weymouth
Designing a multi-functional quiet garden   46

Chapter 5 – Taste and savour   49
Garden Story 5
St Mary's Church of England Primary School, Pulborough
How a garden became the heart of the school   54

Reflections   59

Acknowledgements   60

Seen and unseen
Sound and silence
Touch and feel
Scent and sensing
Taste and savour

Introduction

Primary schools are invariably vibrant, purposeful and immensely inspiring places to be. Staff work tirelessly to provide stimulating and creative environments in which children can become self-motivated and independent learners. Increasingly, in both church and community schools, these environments have included quiet areas where children are able to take time to reflect on their learning, to think about challenges they are facing or to pray.

A good indication of the growing interest in developing spiritual spaces has been the popularity of the *Pause for Reflection* publication (Jumping Fish 2004). This provides practical ways to encourage children's spiritual development through interactive reflection corners. Having witnessed the impact of indoor quiet spaces, schools are now looking to create complimentary areas outside in their grounds. Often these places are taking the form of sensory spiritual gardens and are either used informally by children during break and lunchtimes or by whole class groups for acts of collective worship, circle time and other reflective activities.

This book has been produced in response to many enquiries from teachers keen to know about 'works in progress' in other schools which might provide inspiration or practical help and guidance. I am therefore very grateful to the five

schools that have been willing, with genuine openness and honesty, to share their Garden Stories which give a real insight into the challenges and rewards involved in creating a spiritual garden from scratch. In addition to the Garden Stories each of the main chapters of the book focuses on one of the five senses and explores how planting, art installations, hard landscaping and reflective activities have been used in creative and stimulating ways in primary schools across the country.

If Bertrand Russell is right when he suggests that *'Spirituality is ...the strangeness and wonder lying just below the surface, even in the commonest things'* then it follows that a bit of 'digging' will be needed! Teachers are now reclaiming the wisdom that if children are to marvel at and cherish the created world of which they are a part, then they must be allowed to engage with it at every opportunity. They must plant seeds by hand and watch them grow, feel woodlice scampering through their fingers and worms wriggling on their palms, identify the birds that they see and hear day by day and recognise and value each changing season of the year. This book is therefore unapologetically hands-on in its approach. The suggestions for helping children to reflect on and pray about the world in which they live are multi-sensory, interactive and most importantly designed to be done out of doors.

It has been a huge privilege to observe and record the ways in which many schools are already working in partnership with parents, governors, local businesses, churches, horticultural groups and a host of others to transform the green and grey deserts surrounding their buildings into diverse, creative, sensory spaces where children can discover more about the natural world, each other and themselves.

Seen and uns

When time is given for children to stand and stare at the intricate design of the commonest mini-beast or garden flower, their natural curiosity and sense of wonder can transform the simplest experience from the mundane into the profound.

CHAPTER ONE

Seen and unseen

Pausing to look

Mini signposts can be placed in the garden on which some of the following suggestions are written. The signs should be changed from time to time to maintain children's curiosity and interest.

Look for any changes in the garden since you were last here.

Look very closely at the structure, colours and patterns of the plants.

Look for any mini-beasts creeping, crawling or jumping in the undergrowth.

Look for clues that there is a breeze blowing in the garden – how does it move the different plants?

Look for any birds in the garden, notice their plumage. Can you identify them?

Look for patterns made by shadows if the sun is shining.

Look away from the sun at the sky. Are there clouds today? What kinds of clouds are they? How and where are they moving?

Reflection and prayer

Prayer pool

A pool, which may either be a large bird bath or simply a bowl with a dark interior, can be placed in the garden with appropriate words displayed close by. As the children study their reflection in the water, remind them that God has created each of them with great care and loves them exactly as they are. Invite each child to silently say thank you to God for something they like about themself.

"You are precious in my sight." Isaiah 43.4

The sundial

This could either be a conventional free-standing sundial or created on the ground so that a child standing in the centre casts the shadow, which tells the time. As they focus on the shadow slowly charting the progress of time through the day, ask the children to consider how they will use the hours left to them. What will they feel proud of doing today as they think back before falling asleep?

"This is the day that the Lord has made." Psalm 118.24

Prayer flags

Following a Tibetan tradition, children can write their prayers on prayer flags that can be strung around the garden from trees or fencing. When the flags flutter in the breeze, it is believed that the prayers are blown by the wind into the very presence of God.

"Tell God what you need and thank Him for all he has done." Philippians 4.6

Hard landscaping

Working with the children on designing the structure of your spiritual garden is a vital first step. Often, schools bid for funding so that they can employ a garden designer to help the children make their aspirations and plans a reality. In this chapter's Garden Story garden designer Angela Mould gives an insight into how professional designers work with their brief. Even if, and perhaps especially if, space is at a premium, the design and structure must be simple and clear in order to avoid an over busy, muddled visual impression.

Entrances are important to welcome those approaching the garden. At Field Court Junior School in Gloucester the entrance delineates the end of the playground area and the beginning of the quiet garden, indicating a different type of space and a different code of behaviour. St Osmund's Catholic Primary School in Salisbury wanted the entrance to their garden to be mysterious and secretive. The children chose a winding path to lead people into a peaceful, restful place.

At Sarum St Paul's Primary School in Salisbury Angela Mould designed a grass snail for children to clamber over, which adds interest to the garden by introducing different levels.

The millennium celebrations were the stimulus for St Mary's Catholic School in Bath to create its quiet garden with a beautiful pond for the children to enjoy. They are lucky enough to have a grassy woodland area but wanted a paved all-weather space. Raised beds make the garden boundaries and provide extra seating.

Art and inspiration

Artists are often commissioned by town planners to create pieces that will enhance public spaces and inspire local residents and passers by. Schools are learning from these initiatives and seeking out grants and special funding to enable them to invite artists to work with children on projects that will make their outside areas as visually vibrant and stimulating as the interior.

Children from Sarum St Paul's Primary School in Salisbury worked with a local artist using 'found' pieces of wood to create fantastical creatures, which appear unexpectedly around corners and from under bushes.

St Mary's Primary School in Pulborough covered their otherwise rather boring wooden trellis with home-made, coated papier mâché insects. Another artist was inspired by the pond areas to create a hovering dragonfly. "The children are still totally captivated by it" says headteacher Alyson Heath.

At Beechcroft St Paul's Primary, Weymouth two concrete feet point the way into their garden and the children's printed silk sails add movement and colour.

St Osmund's Catholic Primary School in Salisbury painted signs for the different areas in their garden.

A bamboo tunnel at Sarum St Paul's Primary School.

Painted wall at St Osmund's Primary School.

The rabbit – one of the 'found' wooden creatures at Sarum St Paul's.

Wickerwork sculptures at Beechcroft St Paul's Primary School.

A mosaic sign decorates a wall at St Mary's Primary School Pulborough.

The totem pole at Sarum St Paul's is at the centre of the garden and was carved by a local artist with images from creation.

Planting

Plants for visual impact all year round

When planning the planting, visit a local garden centre or perhaps invite a plant specialist into school to talk to children about the range of plants that will suit the soil type and position of your garden.

A multi-sensory garden should be a feast for the eyes in every season, from the delicate fresh shades of spring to the deep vibrant colours of summer, the burnished oranges and golds of autumn through to the evergreens and architectural plants you will need to make the most of those crisp, frosty mornings.

Plants that attract insects

Children have a natural fascination with every kind of creeping, jumping, hovering or darting creature. But as well as evoking wonderment and awe in humans, it is essential to attract insects into the garden for other important reasons. Insects form a crucial link in the food chain of many native wild creatures as well as being essential in their role as plant pollinators.

Children may be given the opportunity to engage in some research about which plants would be most attractive to insects. Grown in the same proximity, garden plants that yield nectar and pollen can provide a continual food supply for wildlife, from primroses in early spring through to sedum in autumn.

Ideally invite a wildlife expert into school to advise the children about the most suitable insect attracting plants for local soil conditions.

The following list includes plants that will not only attract insects and birds but will also engage all five senses. For example, many have attractive or interesting scent, tactile foliage, striking structure or can be used in cooking.

Annuals

Candytuft *(Iberis umbellata)*
Cornflower *(Centaurea cyanus)*
Sweet Pea *(Lathyrus odoratus)*

Garden shrubs

Buddleia *(Buddleia davidii* or *buddleia globosa)*
Forsythia *(Forsythia intermedia)*
Hebe *(Hebe* spp.*)*
Lavender *(Lavendula spica* var.*)*
Rosemary *(Rosemarinus officinalis)*
Weigela *(Weigela florida)*

Biennials

Honesty *(Lunaria annua)*
Sweet William *(Dianthus barbatus)*
Wallflower *(Cheiranthus cheiri)*

Border perennials

Catmint *(Nepeta cataria)*
Golden Rod *(Solidago* spp.*)*
Hollyhock *(Alcea rosea)*
Michaelmas Daisy *(Aster novi-belgii)*
Primrose *(Primula vulgaris)*
Sedum *(Sedum spectabile)*
Thyme *(Thymus serpyllum* or *Thymus drucei)*

GARDEN STORY 1

Sarum St Paul's Church of England Primary School, Salisbury
Working with a professional garden designer

The project context

Angela Mould completed her training in garden design at Sparsholt College in Hampshire in June 2008. She was approached by Sarum St Paul's Primary School in November 2007 to consider designing a sensory garden for reflection and quiet play.

She writes, "Mr Gentry and Miss Day (two teachers at the school) had already undertaken an extensive two-part consultation with the children. This involved asking them to show, on a simple plan of the school grounds, areas they enjoyed and areas that made them feel unsafe or unwelcome. The children were then asked for more detailed designs to include ideas for hard landscaping and planting."

"Mr Gentry and Miss Day submitted an outline of the project to governors for their approval, put in a bid for lottery funding and contacted the local supermarket for sponsorship."

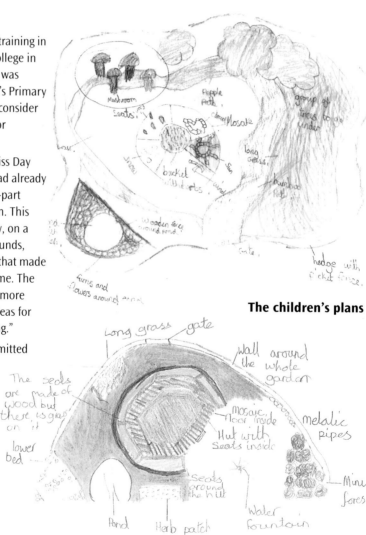

The children's plans

"The work done by the teachers in gathering the ideas and aspirations of the children was invaluable. I had already undertaken my own research as part of an earlier project on school gardens and two themes predominated from all the children's responses:

- The desire for a quiet place or a space set apart.

- The concept of a private or 'secret' garden with a definite entrance to demarcate the garden from the outside world.

Almost all the children said that they did not want football to dominate playtimes to the exclusion of other activities. I was really impressed with the maturity and creativity of the children's responses."

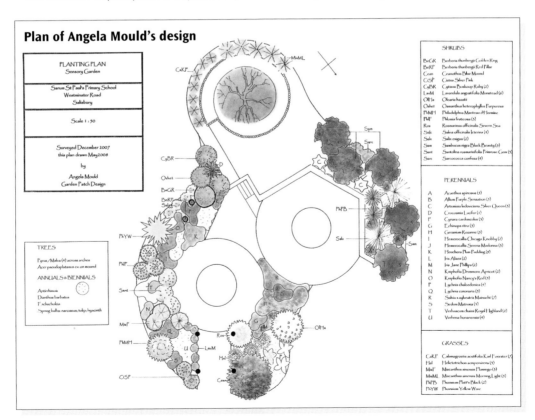

Plan of Angela Mould's design

The learning curve

The project at Sarum St Paul's was one of my first commissions. It is helpful to look back and reflect on what I learnt.

- Determine at the outset who is in charge of the project and who controls the budget.

- Make sure as many people as possible see and understand the design. (When the garden was being built staff realised the cobbled area was a health and safety risk, resulting in the whole area being radically modified!)

- If parents and/or other volunteers are going to help, clear guidelines must be established.

- Do not underestimate the time and cost implications of jobs like earth removal.

- Make sure there is adequate seating – ideally enough for a whole class to use the space.

- The issue of how the garden will be maintained must be addressed BEFORE the start of the project.

Mrs Maureen Morris with her class in the garden.

The 'snail' feature under construction and when completed.

The rewards

- Working to a design brief created by children was challenging but hugely rewarding when they saw their dreams become a reality. The children love the garden. It is so popular that a rota of classes has needed to be drawn up to determine who uses it when. However, it is still a novelty and we hope that a more relaxed approach can be taken in time.

- I had underestimated the visual impact of the garden from inside the school building as well as outside. Teachers tell me that it has really transformed their 'outlook'.

- I am thrilled by the way the garden is being used outside school hours as well as during the day.

- A request was put out for children to volunteer to join a gardening club to help maintain the garden. The numbers responding were higher than for any other club the school has run.

Views of the finished spiritual garden.

Sound and sile

Many children's lives are filled with a cacophony of noise from the moment they wake to the strains of breakfast TV to the time the DVD is switched off in their bedroom (often after they are asleep). Computer games, CDs, iPods and radios fill whatever quiet time remains. Spaces for silence, focused careful listening and quiet reflection will, for thousands of children, only be possible at school.

CHAPTER TWO
Sound and silence

Pausing to listen

Mini signposts can be placed in the garden.

Listen for sounds very close to you, coming from within the garden.

Listen for sounds coming from outside the garden, perhaps from the school building.

Listen for faraway sounds. Can you guess who or what is making the sounds?

Listen for a new sound that you have never heard before. Try to focus in on that one sound only.

Listen for the bird song. Is it possible to see the birds that you can hear?

Listen for the rustle and whispering of leaves or other plants being blown by the breeze.

Reflection and prayer

Have some wind chimes in your garden. As the wind moves the chimes they touch each other and make beautiful sounds. A garden is a lovely place to gather and make music together.

"Sing to God with thanksgiving in your heart."
Colossians 3.16

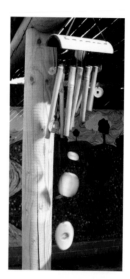

Children are intrigued when they hold a shell to their ear for the first time and hear the sound of the sea. As they listen, encourage them to allow their imaginations to transport them to a far away seashore, where they can taste the spray from the ocean waves on their tongues, hear the cry of the gulls in the air, smell the seaweed and imagine the fine golden sand running through their fingers. God has created a wonderful world for us to enjoy with all our senses. Ask the children if there are other sounds that make them think of special places.

"Be still and know that I am God." Psalm 46.10

The sense of hearing can help children to pray for others. Invite them to close their eyes and listen to sounds far off and pray for someone who lives some distance away, someone they would like to see more, someone who needs their prayers.

Now ask them to listen to voices from within the school building and pray for someone they know in school who is unhappy or struggling. Finally encourage them to concentrate on the sound of their own steady breathing and pray for themselves; for anything that they are concerned or nervous about.

"Do not worry about anything, but pray about everything." Philippians 4.6

Planting

Plants to listen to

Gardens are seldom completely silent because
even the faintest breeze will rustle leaves, rattle
seed pods, make grasses whisper and set bamboo
clacking. When the children begin to plan their
garden, remind them to consider how they would
like the garden to sound as well as how they
want it to look. Ask advice from a specialist about
plants which sound interesting when there is a
breeze.

Rustling grasses at Wool First Primary School.
Honesty (Lunaria annua).
Bamboo (Phyllostachys aurea).

Art and inspiration

As well as enjoying the sounds of plants, birds and insects in the garden, some schools have sensitively sited other 'instruments' and features to lift the spirits.

At Hope Brook Primary School an artist was commissioned to create some stunning, giant instruments for a paved garden area. These make very beautiful sounds and are quite safe for children to use unsupervised.

At St Osmund's Catholic Primary School natural woods and bamboos have been used to make xylophones and glockenspiels, which create gentle, mellow music in their secret garden.

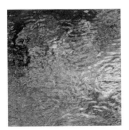

Using water in the garden

Perhaps the sound most associated with relaxation and calm is that of running, trickling, splashing or dripping water. Beechcroft St Paul's Primary School, Weymouth has two water features. The first is shaped like two exotic birds, which alternately nod their heads as water trickles from their beaks. The second has water running smoothly down three steel posts making them glisten and gleam in the sunlight. The head-teacher, Sarah Sprague, says that the features have been the stimulus for some wonderful poetry written by the children.

Flowforms (above right) are wonderful for making watery sounds as the water takes a circular course through each level.

The water features at Beechcroft St Paul's Primary School.

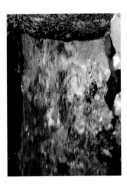

Seating and perches

Encouraging children to be still for a while to listen attentively to the sounds around them is much easier when there is plenty of comfortable, dry and accessible seating.

Sarum St Paul's Primary School, in Salisbury, brightened up a corner of their garden with a mural and a shelter, enabling the garden to be used in all weathers.

St Mary's Primary School, Pulborough has made the most of the available central space in their St Mary's garden by using an angular bench engraved with the Lord's Prayer. Also in their garden, they have a story chair on which children can sit to tell stories to friends during morning and lunch breaks.

Many schools have worked with willow artists to create domes, tunnels and all kinds of other structures. The example shown above has a paved area inside so that children can sit in the igloo even when the grass is wet.

A gift of money to Wool First School funded the arbour seat, which blends well with the other natural materials used in their garden. A low retaining wall around raised beds provides more perch space for children. In contrast a hexagonal design has been used for the garden seating at Field Court Junior School.

St Mary's Catholic Primary School in Bath has a number of established broadleaved trees in their woodland garden, which provide cool shade over the benches where children can gather on warm days and listen to the leaves rustling above them.

The colourful 'friendship bench' at Gastrells School in Gloucestershire was given so that children could remember a former pupil, Scott, who died tragically and is badly missed. Children can go and sit on the bench when they want to think about him.

The 'story chair' at St Mary's, Pulborough.

Hard landscaping

Sound and surface materials

A variety of surfaces, such as bark chipping, paving, different sizes of gravel and cobbles can be used for auditory impact in the garden.

These cobbles at Hartpury Church of England Primary School symbolise the Trinity and incorporate the children's mosaic fishes around the swirling periphery of the Celtic design.

Bark slats and wired sticks are used for fencing at Beechcroft St Paul's Primary School garden.

28

Attracting wildlife

Birds

A peaceful spiritual garden is a perfect place to actively encourage birds to come and make their home. Children will not only appreciate their beautiful and evocative songs but may also learn in time to identify the different native species. The needs of garden birds are very simple – shelter, food, water and nesting sites.

Shelter: Birds need cover to escape predators and afford protection against wind and rain. Thorny plants will give such protection and evergreens will provide some covering during the cold winter months.

Food: Plants that provide natural food in the form of seeds and fruits, and plants that attract insects, are ideal. Native varieties are generally preferred. A pile of dead wood will harbour insects and so provide a plentiful food supply. Blackbirds, thrushes and some other species prefer open areas of mown grass in which to feed. During very cold and frosty weather when natural food sources are scarce, artificial foods such as kitchen scraps can be a life saver to birds. However, it is vitally important that these are provided every day without fail as birds quickly become dependent on them. A break in supply could mean death to a small bird. Suitable artificial foods should only be given during the winter (November to March), never in spring and summer as some of it could be lethal if fed to nestlings.

Nest Boxes: At Beechcroft St Paul's Primary School in Weymouth pupils had great fun designing and making their own nest boxes to place around school grounds as well as in their multi-sensory garden. They researched the optimum size of boxes for different species as well as the best places in which to site the boxes (i.e. not exposed to prevailing winds, rain or sun and out of reach of predators).

GARDEN STORY 2

Wool Church of England First School, Wool
A Spiritual Garden: A place set apart for reflection and worship

Wool First School is set in a thriving rural community and is situated next to the Parish Church. When the old school house became vacant, headteacher Lesley Craze saw an opportunity! She and the governors suggested that some of the extensive garden could be retained and used by the school.

The position of the garden together with its established boundary hedging and walls immediately caught the children's imagination and it became known as 'The Spiritual Garden'.

The 'tucked away' nature of the garden meant that it could not be easily supervised by the members of staff on playground duty. It was therefore decided to keep the garden as a special place for quiet, reflective activities. Open air worship is now regularly held here and the covered shelter, called the Summer House, can hold a whole class for sharing activities or circle time. The garden has been designed with lots of nooks and crannies. The Head and other members of staff often visit the garden when they need a few peaceful moments to draw breath. "In a way our garden is like an outside church and is very much a sacred space", says Mrs Craze.

The entrance to 'The Spiritual Garden'.

The Summer House.

The deputy head Catherine Dalgleish who has also worked hard to establish the garden says, "We have tried to involve the community in the project as much as possible and a local firm, working in partnership with the British Trust for Conservation Volunteers (BTCV), sent 20 of its workers for 2 days to help us with the heavy jobs. A gift from the church was given from profits made on the Parish Magazine and with this the sundial and arbour seat were purchased. Another grant paid for the tiny engraved stone Celtic cross which is often our focus when we have outdoor collective worship.

Another teacher has a team of children who help her maintain the garden. The theme of the garden is 'growth'. Just as we care for the plants to help them grow, we also believe here at Wool that we should be providing the right conditions for our children to grow not just physically and intellectually but emotionally and spiritually as well."

Wool children enjoying their 'Spiritual Garden'.

Touch and

As young babies, children make sense of the world through touch. Many child development specialists believe that the modern obsession with hygiene, health and safety, albeit well-intentioned, is slowly alienating children from the natural world, which was created for them to explore and enjoy.

CHAPTER THREE
Touch and feel

Pausing to touch

Mini signposts can be placed in the garden.

Touch gently three different leaves in the garden; perhaps a shiny smooth leaf, a soft furry leaf and a pointy sharp leaf. Look around at the amazing variety of colours, textures and shapes of foliage.

Touch the soil. The temperature of the soil tells gardeners about the growing conditions for plants. Is the soil heavy and solid or light and crumbly?

Touch the breeze with an outstretched hand or an upturned face. Can you decide the direction that the wind is coming from?

Touch water somewhere in the garden. Is it cold or has it been warmed by the sun?

Touch two or three things in the garden made of wood. Lightly run your hands over their surfaces. Wood comes from trees. Trees are essential to life on our planet. Feel the texture of the bark on different trees.

Touch the cold surfaces of some stones or rocks. If they are not too heavy lift them up and take a look at what is underneath. Remember to replace them.

Reflection and prayer

The Treasure Chest: Place a wicker picnic basket in the garden containing a selection of natural objects such as feathers, cones, shells, seeds, pebbles and pieces of bark. Children can be invited to close their eyes, lift the lid of the basket, take out one thing to handle carefully and describe its shape, texture and temperature before replacing it. Explain that for some people the sense of touch is their only way of 'seeing' the world and it is the sense that perhaps we most take for granted.

"Split a piece of rock and I am there, lift a piece of stone and you will find me there." **Gnostic Gospel of St Thomas**

Use the spokes of a bicycle wheel or a wooden trellis to create a weaving frame. Take the class on a nature walk to collect natural materials (or invite them to bring something from the natural world to school) to weave into or tie onto the frame. When every child has added something, suggest that the weaving represents the class. It is complete only when there is something from every member. As the children look at the leaves, cones, feathers and berries they can thank God for the contribution that each one of them makes to the group.

"God saw all that He had made and it was very good."
Genesis 1.31

Place several trays of sand in the garden so that children can make their own miniature gardens from leaves, twigs and pebbles (or anything else they can find around the grounds). Then tell a version of the creation story in Genesis chapters 1 and 2 and ask the children what they imagine the Garden of Eden might have been like.

"The Lord God planted a garden in the East, in Eden."
Genesis 2.8

Art and inspiration

Art designed for schools needs to work in a range of different ways. The pieces should be tactile as well as visually exciting to encourage children to explore them in a multi-sensory way.

The sculpture at Tutshill Primary School is loved by the children for its imposing size and the way they can sit in, stand on and swing round it.

The metal snail at St Mary's Primary School, Pulborough sits near the pond. It is durable in the winter weather and has withstood hundreds of pats, strokes and rubs over the years. It also crops up regularly in children's own artwork and creative writing.

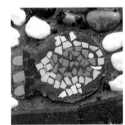

Mosaic art can bring visual impact to otherwise bland, uninteresting surfaces. It is very popular in schools because many children have the opportunity to contribute to the design, giving them a common sense of ownership and pride. The fish design is a detail from the Trinity mosaic at Hartpury Primary School in Gloucestershire.

A school badge mosaic is the centrepiece of the paved area in the Millennium garden at St Mary's Primary School in Bath.

Planting

Plants with tactile foliage

Some plants seem to have been especially created to be stroked or gently run though the fingers.

Grasses not only look beautiful as they sway and whisper in the breeze but some are also wonderfully light and feathery to the touch. Lambs' Ears *(Stachys byzantina)* feel exactly like fine velvet and are a perennial favourite with children.

Chinese Lanterns *(Physalis alkekengi)* are as delicate and translucent as tissue paper and bring texture as well as sound to the garden. In contrast thistles *(Eryngium bourgatii)*, globe artichokes *(Cynara cardunculus)* and holly *(Ilex aquifolum)*, with their pointy sharp spikes, demonstrate the breathtaking variety that can be achieved in the careful use of foliage in a multi-sensory garden.

Choose five or six distinctive leaves and place each one in a feelie bag. Invite the children to guess the name of each leaf by using touch only.

Healing and wholeness

The title of this chapter is Touch and Feel because since ancient times gardens have been visited by people who feel in need of spiritual inspiration and physical healing.

Many herbal preparations are straightforward and safe to make in class and support work in Science and PSHE on keeping healthy. A local homeopath could be invited into school to talk about how remedies are derived from plants and other natural materials to make effective treatments for common ailments.

Alternatively, bring in a variety of healing plants and herbs to let the children enjoy the smell as they are touched.

Hypericum (top) and common garden herbs – sage (right), oregano (far right), thyme (below right) and borage (below far right).

Attracting wildlife

Mini-beasts

Many schools now have wild areas in their grounds which may include ponds. The safety issues associated with deep water often result in the area being fenced off and only used by the children when they have adult supervision. Most of the time children cannot get close enough to touch the mini-beasts that will certainly live here.

One solution is to develop a corner of your garden as a mini-beast habitat. To do this plant wild flowers, grasses and nettles for butterflies and spiders, put a few rotting logs around for beetles and earwigs and a pile of old bricks, flower pots or broken slabs to provide nooks and crannies for snails and woodlice. A flat bowl dug into the ground and filled with water may even attract waterboatmen, pond snails, great diving beetles or daphnia. Plenty of mini-beasts in your garden will also have the added bonus of attracting more birds, so a little untidiness may pay dividends.

Earthworms

Earthworms are vital creatures to have in the garden for several reasons. As they eat their way through the soil in search of dead plant material they break up the hard lumps of earth, making it easier for the gardener to work. Worms are also an important food source for birds. The more you can encourage worms by leaving some dead material on the surface of the ground the more birds will visit your garden.

Making a wormery: Even in the smallest garden there will be many hundreds, if not thousands, of worms; however, it is clearly difficult for the children to study their movements because they spend most of their time underground. A wormery with transparent perspex walls will enable the children to study the amazing way in which worms move soil about. The wormery needs to contain layers of different soils divided by gravel and have a few dead leaves on the surface.

Worm watching: Worms usually come out at night. Children can encourage them to the surface in the day if they gently tap their feet on the ground for around five minutes (mimicking the birds, which tap or peck at the ground to simulate rain).

Worm listening: To listen to the worms children should take a moist piece of paper and place it on a flat, stable surface in the garden. Lay a worm on the paper and watch as it contracts and spreads its muscles to move along. By placing their ear near the paper, children will be able to hear the scratching sound of the bristles. The bristles help the worm to grip the edges of its burrows and also make a useful anchor if a bird is trying to pull it out of the ground.

GARDEN STORY 3

St Osmund's Catholic Primary School, Salisbury
A whole school project to develop the outside space

St Osmund's Catholic Primary School is situated in the centre of the city, adjacent to blocks of flats and bordered by two busy and very noisy roads. Several years ago a team of staff and parents had a vision to create a haven within the walls of St Osmund's School. Their aim was to provide a series of different spaces in which children, whose lives were normally full of clamour and noise, could go for imaginative play, peace and reflection.

The site of the school, though not large and with no playing field, had several areas that were not being fully utilised. There were also a number of mature trees that could provide shade and shelter if the area around them was cleared and made safe.

Mr Barton, who teaches at the school, explains how the project was approached.

"The team of parent helpers asked each class to choose an area within the grounds and say how they would like to see it transformed. There was of course great excitement and discussion about possible themes and a process of collaboration about design and materials began. Some of the ideas were pretty ambitious but the parents went to enormous lengths to realise the children's dreams.

The Reception Class asked for a magical garden which could be inhabited by fairies and elves when the children went home.

Class 1 wanted a secret garden with a curved path leading into a leafy private space for quiet conversations.

The magical garden.

Quiet conversation in the leafy space.

The covered seating area.

Noah's ark playground wall painting.

The outdoor worship space.

Another group wanted to sow and harvest their own crops and designed raised beds with mosaic surrounds. Each child chose objects of interest or significance to them and set them in cement.

Some of the children thought that the grounds needed a covered seating area, where a whole class could go to be outside for circle time, even in the rain! Others asked that the drab walls which surrounded the school boundary be painted to bring colour and interest. Scenes from Bible stories were chosen."

Another staff member, Mrs Jean Banks, had noticed a small space which had been enclosed by a new building extension. It was overlooked by a classroom and a corridor and had real potential to be redesigned for outdoor worship. "We paved and planted the area and now I lead a service of prayer and reflection during lunchtimes in the summer months for any children who want to take part. We would like to develop the area further and encourage the children to use it as an outside chapel every break but as it's a bit tucked away we are struggling to ensure adequate supervision."

"The redevelopment of our outside grounds has had a huge impact on the quality of children's experience during breaks and lunch times", said Mr Barton, "and because everyone has had a hand in its design there is a real corporate pride in what we have created. There are rarely behavioural issues at break times now because of all the different areas in which the children can play."

Scent and sens

Gardens are places where children can be introduced to a wide variety of natural aromas that may be new to them, like the perfume of wallflowers and narcissi in spring or the distinctive smells of culinary and therapeutic herbs. Spiritual gardens are increasingly used by schools for acts of collective worship, where the smell of incense or burning perfumed oils can add to the multi-sensory experience.

CHAPTER FOUR

Scent and sensing

Pausing to smell

Mini signposts can be placed in the garden.

Smell the earth by holding a handful of soil and rubbing its crumbly texture between your fingers.

Smell any flowers that are in bloom in your garden.

Smell the compost or leaf mould heap. Well-rotted compost smells rich and earthy. This precious material will give life and strength to next season's plants.

Smell the time of day! Often there are smells associated with the freshness of a morning, the heavier richer smells as the sun beats down on the plants at midday. The breeze sometimes has a special smell and so does the frost in winter. After a shower of rain the garden will smell its very best.

Smell the herbs in the garden by passing your fingers through the leaves or gently pressing them. Can you name them and remember how they can be used?

Smell the aromas from outside the garden. Can you identify them – grass being cut, smoke from fires, food being cooked, fumes from factories or cars?

Reflection and prayer

A healing gift

Lavender has been valued for its healing properties since Greek and Roman times. It is an essential plant for spiritual gardens. Each child could be invited to pick one stem to stick on a prayer card made for someone who is unwell.

"Scents and fragrant oils make you feel happier."
Proverbs 27.9

Symbolic gifts

Read to the children the account of the presentation of the wise men's gifts to the infant Jesus in Matthew's gospel. Explain that each of the gifts had a symbolic meaning and was precious at that time. Burn three or four different perfumed oils or incense sticks and ask which of the fragrances the children like best. Does their favourite fragrance make them think of a colour, feeling or experience they have had?

"…they opened their treasures and presented him with gifts of gold, and of frankincense and of myrrh."
Matthew 2.11

A precious gift

Mary was not a wealthy woman but she brought a gift of costly perfume to honour Jesus. Ask the children which gift they would choose to give to Jesus.

"Mary took about a pint of pure nard, an expensive perfume; she poured it on Jesus' feet and wiped his feet with her hair." John 12.3

Planting

Aromatic plants

When planning your sensory garden it is always helpful to take advice about plants that will not only provide year-round visual interest but also have a natural scent or perfume. As well as garden flowers such as geranium *(Geraniaceae)*, honeysuckle *(Lonicera periclymenum)* and tobacco plant *(Nicotiana alata)* there are also many aromatic species that have a range of therapeutic properties. The following examples can easily be grown in the garden, but it may be useful to buy the oils so that their qualities can be experienced by the children.

Rosemary *(Rosmarinus officinalis)* essential oil is said to promote clear thinking, aid concentration and improve the memory. Spearmint *(Mentha spicata)* essential oil counteracts tiredness and encourages more positive thinking in those who are feeling low. French Marigold *(Tagetes patula)* essential oil is an aromatic oil often used by athletes to refresh tired feet.

Invite an aromatherapist into school to talk to the children about how they use plants to make their preparations.

GARDEN STORY 4

Beechcroft St Paul's Church of England Primary School, Weymouth
Designing a multi-functional quiet garden

Beechcroft St Paul's Primary School is situated in the centre of a large area of social housing on the outskirts of Weymouth. Space is at a premium but when she became headteacher in 2005 Sarah Sprague identified a good-sized triangular area at the side of the school, which was used only as a walkway.

"I was so excited because I felt what was really lacking in the school was a place in which children could just go to chill out and enjoy a creative, stimulating environment. I love the creative arts myself and I dreamt of making a place in which creativity of every kind could flourish.

We have a Teaching Assistant who is passionate about growing things and we had no space for a garden in school so we created raised beds, one for each class to manage through the year. We made a decked stage (or rather my husband came in one summer holiday and made it) and we used railway sleepers for a seating area. There are plenty of them so that children can either use them to sit and chat together at break times or they can watch performances during lessons or worship. The one shown on the next page is a performance of the Good Samaritan shared as part of a class's own act of worship. We have musical concerts in the garden and all kinds of drama."

Circle time in the garden.

A summer house is situated in the playground.

Seating areas, bird feeders and raised beds with vegetables, herbs and other plants.

"The space is also the presentation space for pieces of visual art like willow weaving or painted fabric sails. We try to attract birds to the area by providing feeding stations, a bird bath and nest boxes. Some of the children at Beechcroft St Paul's Primary School don't have gardens at home so this has become a kind of special sacred place. We have wind chimes and water fountains to try to foster a feeling of calm and peace. For many of us here, this is our favourite place in the whole school and certainly the place where we feel closest to God."

A performance of the Good Samaritan.

Taste and sa

Schools are now opening up parts of their grounds to grow all kinds of produce so that children can discover the joys of eating food that they themselves have sown, tended and harvested. What better place to hold a Harvest Festival celebration than outside in your spiritual garden?

CHAPTER FIVE

Taste and savour

Pausing to taste and savour

Mini signposts can be placed in the garden.

Taste and savour your fruit at break time in a new way by eating outside in the garden. Close your eyes and eat it a piece at a time. What do you notice about the flavours and textures that you had not been aware of before?

Taste some of the food that has been grown in your garden and cooked in school. Taste happens on different parts of your tongue. For example, bitter tastes (like the taste of tonic water) are mostly sensed towards the back and rear sides of the tongue. Salty tastes and sweet tastes (like sugar) are tasted at the tip of the tongue and sour tastes (like lemon juice) are mostly tasted at the sides, middle and towards the front of the tongue.

Taste some of the different herbs that you have grown in your garden. Try to remember their names and the foods they compliment.

Taste samples of food and try to identify what they are. Prepare two sets of five small chunks of different fruit and vegetables. Choose two children who enjoy eating fresh fruit and vegetables and place a blindfold on each. As they guess the food, record their success rate and see who wins!

Reflection and prayer

Children are often in school during Holy Week and traditional foods like hot cross buns and chocolate eggs can be used to reflect on aspects of this most special season of the Church year.

The Symbol of the Cross

Explain to the children that long ago only wealthy people had the chance of an education. Symbols and pictures were important in helping people to learn about Bible stories. Ask the children to gather twigs, stones or leaves and use them to make the shape of a cross on the ground as a focus for reflection.

Jesus went to a garden on the night before he died because he wanted to be alone with God and pray. He knew that he had to face the cross and asked for strength to do God's will.

It is traditional that on Good Friday buns are baked with the symbol of the cross on the top as a reminder of the way that Jesus died. Share hot cross buns among the children and after a few moments of quiet read John 19.16-17. An appropriate song like *The Servant King* may be sung.

"Pilate had a notice prepared and fastened to the cross. It read: Jesus of Nazareth, the King of the Jews." **John 19.19**

The Garden Tomb

The place where Jesus' body was laid was like a cave carved from the rocky cliff face in the garden of a rich man. A heavy stone sealed the entrance. Use the two halves of a large hollow chocolate egg to symbolise the opening of the tomb as the story of the Resurrection is read from Luke 24.1-7. Afterwards, break the egg into pieces and share amongst the children.

"He is not here, he has risen!" **Luke 24.6**

Planting

Tasty plants

Children at Wool First School *(right)* have enjoyed planting a range of herbs in beds, pots and various corners all over the garden. "We try to use them in the cooking we do in school", says Mrs Dalgleish. "Many of the flavours are quite new to the children and why shouldn't we be educating taste buds as well as minds!"

Take the children into the garden for a herbal tea tasting. Try mint or camomile tea. These can be made using crops grown in the garden but can also be bought from a supermarket and brewed in school.

Children enjoying the herbs growing in raised beds at Beechcroft St Paul's Primary School in Weymouth.

Spiritual celebrations

Religious Education is the curriculum subject that perhaps contributes the most opportunities for developing children's spirituality as they learn about and from the followers of different faith traditions.

The following three Jewish festivals all include the eating of fruit as part of the family celebration.

Sukkot

Each year Jewish people celebrate the festival of Sukkot when they build structures in their gardens, and sometimes on their flat roofs, in which to eat their meals and, in warmer climates, to sleep. They are remembering how their ancestors journeyed in the desert for forty years in search of the special land that God had promised them. Because they were travellers with no fixed home they built shelters, or sukkot, in which to eat and sleep with their families.

Traditionally, the roof of the sukkah (singular of sukkot) is made of leaves and branches with a gap through which to see the stars. Often fruits or pictures of fruits are hung from the walls and roof.

Children could build a simple sukkah in the spiritual garden and on the pictures of fruit write prayers of thanksgiving to God for their favourite fruit.

Children at Oldbury-on-Severn Primary School busy making their Sukkah.

Rosh Hashanah

Rosh Hashanah is the Jewish New Year and the celebrations last two days. Jewish people reflect on the past year and say sorry for the mistakes they have made. New clothes are worn to symbolise a new start and people use the greeting "L'shana tova" which means "to a good year". At the beginning of the evening meal each member of the family will eat a piece of apple dipped in honey. The sweet taste reminds them of the hope that the coming year will be full of good things.

Either as part of the study of Rosh Hashanah in RE or at the start of a new school year, children could go into the garden and follow the Jewish tradition of eating a slice of apple dipped in honey as they talk together about their hopes and dreams for the future.

Tu B'Shevat

Tu B'Shevat occurs in February when the trees in Israel are just beginning to bear fruit. It is celebrated by planting trees and eating fruit. Often people try a fruit that they have not tasted for a long time.

As part of the teaching of Tu B'Shevat children could use a nursery catalogue to research a particular tree that would suit their garden. They could send for it and when it arrives create their own tree-planting ceremony. The celebration could conclude with a tasting session of unusual or exotic fruits.

GARDEN STORY 5

St Mary's Church of England Primary School, Pulborough
How a garden became the heart of the school

How a garden helped to create an ethos

When Alyson Heath arrived at St Mary's Primary School in 2003 the school had been through some difficult times. Behaviour at break times was a cause for concern and the number of reports recorded in the 'incidents book' was steadily rising. The school was under-performing in various ways which was contributing to the falling roll year on year. The school serves a mixed catchment area and parents were choosing not to send their children to their local school.

Alyson takes up the story.

"Despite some of the school's difficulties there were some huge things working in its favour. As well as some extremely committed staff members and a supportive church community, the school buildings, set in extensive grounds, had significant potential. However, the outside environment was at that time very barren. I began by asking the children why they thought break times weren't working very well. There were several recurring themes that emerged from their responses: there was 'nothing to do', 'football takes over everything and if you don't want to play there are no alternatives' and 'if you want to just chat or even read something, there is nowhere to go'. I also noticed something a bit more subtle, which was perhaps more to do with what the children didn't say. It seemed to me that other than some don'ts, like 'Don't Bully' and 'Don't use bad language', there were no commonly held moral, social and

The early stages of planning and organising the garden.

*Making the garden –
work in progress.*

spiritual imperatives coming through. I began to ask some fundamental questions: What did St Mary's Primary School stand for? What united us? What did we mean to each other? What made us a community?

I came to believe that until these core issues were looked at, it would be difficult to address symptoms like inappropriate behaviour and low morale.

About that time the Gloucester Diocese published 'Values for Life', which provides worship materials to support the teaching of basic Christian values such as generosity, service, forgiveness and friendship. This resource acted as a kind of catalyst for the whole school community to look at which values were really at the heart of our school. It provided a common language that we could use to talk about those rather intangible but none the less very real issues around the beliefs and guiding principles that we all held. Together we began to articulate a vision for our school and during an away day at a local retreat centre we explored how that vision would be expressed in every part of our life at St Mary's Primary School. Everyone agreed that if behaviour was to improve at break times we needed to take seriously the children's comments about the outside space. The first task was to create plenty of seating, so that everyone could sit down if they wanted to. Football was restricted to one area of the playground and I asked parents (many of whom had not had good experiences of school themselves) to help Years 1 and 2 create a fantastic vegetable garden."

Working together on the project

"The local horticultural society helped us by providing plants to fill troughs and planters around the school. We managed to secure funding to commission artists and craftsmen to work with the children to create pieces of art, which helped to make the outside environment more stimulating and interesting.

Without doubt, however, the project that has had most impact on our ethos and the children's sense of pride in the school has been the spiritual garden.

The children wanted an enclosed area 'with a proper entrance' where they could go to read, tell stories to each other or just be quiet and still. We decided to dedicate the garden to St Mary. This was a key decision, because not only did it give us a theme and plenty of inspiration, but it also served to strengthen the links with our local parish church, who were indeed incredibly supportive of the project.

Although everyone in the school contributed in some way to the making of the garden, it was Year 3 India class that led the way. The photographs are from the big book that they made to record progress."

Planting begins.

The garden nears completion.

Making the garden was a genuinely cross-curricular project

MATHEMATICS We measured the perimeter of our garden and measured where we needed to dig the holes for the fence posts.

ICT We used the internet to find out more about the flowers we were going to plant and their links to St Mary.

ART We drew designs for mosaics. We tried to link together Mary, our garden, the church and our school in our designs.

LITERACY We planned out posters and letters to ask people in Pulborough, the local garden society and the church congregation to help us with our garden.

RELIGIOUS EDUCATION We learned about Mary and what she was like as a person. We looked at lots of pictures of her and chose words that described her.

"Part of our research into the history of gardens revealed that in medieval times a garden was not just a pretty, cared for space. The enclosed area was a sacred or spiritual haven which might represent the soul.

This image of the soul has become real for us at St Mary's Primary School. As we have worked together to create the garden, it has become a focus and symbol for our unity. We often hold our worship there and it is the place that children go to sort out problems both within and between themselves. It is everything we dreamt it would be – a quiet, still, sacred refuge at the heart of our school."

Reflections

Visiting schools and spending time with the staff involved in the process of creating the spiritual gardens featured in this book has been hugely rewarding. However, those who speak and write most powerfully about their outdoor spiritual spaces are the children themselves.

The final words are theirs.

"I read my book in there and it feels like God is with me." Jasmine, aged 6

"The garden means a lot to me. I like to relax there and it gets rid of all my nerves." Joshua, aged 8

"I sometimes say a prayer in my head when I am in the garden with my eyes open."
Samson, aged 6

"When I'm in the spiritual garden it's peaceful."
Aleesha-Jade, aged 6

"I like it when our teacher reads us stories in the garden." Callum, aged 7

"I like smelling the plants and feeling the air."
Annabel, aged 6

"I sometimes whistle to the birds in the garden and they sing back to me." Jasmine, aged 7

"The garden is special to our whole school."
Stacey, aged 4

Acknowledgements

The author is extremely grateful to the staff and children of the five schools which allowed their Garden Stories to be told:

Sarum St Paul's Church of England Primary School, Salisbury and their garden designer, Angela Mould.

Wool Church of England First School, Wool, Dorset.

St Osmund's Catholic Primary School, Salisbury.

Beechcroft St Paul's Church of England Primary School, Weymouth.

St Mary's Church of England Primary School, Pulborough, West Sussex.

Thanks also to the following schools for permitting parts of their gardens to be photographed for this book:

Field Court Junior School, Gloucester.

Gastrells Community Primary School, Stroud, Gloucestershire.

Hartpury Church of England Primary School, Gloucestershire.

Hope Brook Church of England Primary School, Longhope, Gloucestershire

Oldbury-on-Severn Church of England Primary School, Thornbury, South Gloucestershire.

St Andrew's Church of England Primary School, Chedworth, Gloucestershire.

St Mary's Catholic Primary School, Bath.

Tutshill Church of England Primary School, Chepstow.

Thanks to Nick Darien-Jones for his superb photographs and the creative and empathetic way that he designed and produced this book.

Additional photography by Shahne Vickery, Jonathan Vickery, Carolyn Wright, Brad Scamp and Corbis.

Above all, thanks are due to Carolyn Wright, Manager of the Gloucester Diocesan RE Resource Centre who worked from my random array of notes, sketches and photographs to assemble this text into some kind of coherent order. Without Carolyn this project would simply not have left the starting blocks.

For *Pause for Reflection* and other Jumping Fish publications contact:

Diocese of Gloucester REsource Centre
Telephone: 01452 835560
Email: jumpingfish@glosdioc.org.uk
Website: www.gloucester.anglican.org